"A THOUGHT FOR THE WEEK"

A Collection of 52
Inspirational Thoughts
to Feed the Mind
And Nourish the Soul

By
Tonia Slaton

Volume I

© 2021

ALL RIGHTS RESERVED. No part of this book may be reproduced in any written, electronic, recording, or photocopying without written permission of the publisher or author. The exception would be in the case of brief quotations embodied in the critical articles or reviews and pages where permission is specifically granted by the publisher or author.

LEGAL DISCLAIMER. Although the author has made every effort to ensure that the information in this book was correct at press time, the author do not assume and hereby disclaim any liability to any party for any loss, damage, or disruption caused by errors or omissions, whether such errors or omissions result from negligence, accident, or any other cause.

Published By: Pen Legacy, LLC
Bible Scriptures Used From King James Version

Library of Congress Cataloging – in- Publication Data has been applied for.

ISBN: 978-1-7370120-0-9

PRINTED IN THE UNITED STATES OF AMERICA.

DEDICATION

This book is dedicated to those of us who have a good heart, want to do good, have done good, want to continue to do good, and have a genuine love for others. Continue to be that person that you are because GOD is watching, and He knows our hearts. I salute you.

Stay prayed up and keep GOD first.

PREFACE

Each day I arrive at work, I pray to my heavenly father that I have a good day, to assist me in guiding my tongue and to allow me to be mindful of my attitude and my actions.

After my 9 to 5 job, I come home, thank God for my job, and then conduct a self-evaluation of my day. It is what I think of my day, how I performed my job, how I interacted with others, and more importantly, have I wronged anyone intentionally or unintentionally.

After my evaluation, if I have decided that I have done my best work that day, have had good interaction with others and have not wronged anyone intentionally or unintentionally, then I have had a good day.

If I feel that I have wronged someone, I know it would not be intentionally, I will make it my business to correct my actions the next day. I take this action even if the person that I have wronged (in my opinion) does not think so or was not aware of my actions towards them. It is how I keep myself, my attitude, and my actions in tack.

This is to shape my week so that I can like what I see when I look in the mirror each day and be at peace when I go to bed at night.

It is my hope that my *Collection of 52 Inspirational Thoughts for the Week* will stimulate the minds and nourish the souls of my readers.

ACKNOWLEDGEMENTS

But they that wait upon the LORD shall renew their strength; they shall mount up with wings as eagles; they shall run, and not be weary; and they shall walk, and not faint. **(Isaiah 40:31 [King James Version])**

God is so awesome, and I am forever grateful for His grace and mercy.

I would like to take the opportunity to acknowledge those who know the be on time, say what you mean and mean what you say, no non-sense Tonia Slaton. No names need to be mentioned because you know who you are. I appreciate the acceptance from you of the real me.

Special acknowledgement goes out to Jermaine Smith. Thank you so much kind sir for lighting the torch for this book. You spoke it and here it is. Your support is greatly appreciated.

"A Thought for the Week"

We are the sum total of our own life experiences

*[10]Each one should
use whatever gift he has
received to serve others, faithfully
administering God's grace
in its various forms.
[11]If anyone speaks, he should
do it as one speaking the very words
of God. If anyone serves, he
should do it with the strength God
provides, so that in all
things God may be praised through
Jesus Christ.
To him be the glory and the power
For ever and ever,
Amen*

**1 Peter 4: 10-11
(New International Version)**

WEEK 1:

Make a list of your passions and dreams. Think back to when you were younger and thought you had all the time in the world. Now pick three things from your list and make them happen. Start living today. Continue to keep God first, stay prayed up, and have a blessed week.

"A Thought for the Week"

²And the LORD answered me, and said, write the vision and make it plain upon tablets, that he may run that readeth it.

(Habakkuk 2:2 [King James Version])

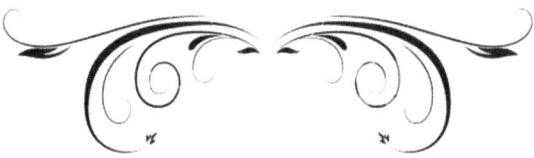

WEEK 2:

Do you like what you see when you look in the mirror? If not, change it. Remember that God gave us free will and life is too short not to have everything that you need and almost everything you want! Continue to keep God first, stay prayed up, and have a blessed week.

¹⁸But we all, with open face beholding as in a glass the glory of the LORD, are changed into the same image from glory to glory, even as by the Spirit of the LORD.

(2 Corinthians 3:18 [King James Version])

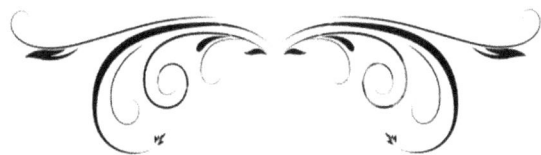

WEEK 3:

Life is so precious and should not be taken for granted. Take a moment to call a friend or loved and just say hello, how are you doing, or I love you because life is too short to leave this earth with regrets. Continue to keep God first, stay prayed up, and have a blessed week.

⁷The end of all things is near; Therefore, be clear minded and self-controlled so that you can pray. ⁸Above all, love each other deeply, because love covers over a multitude of sin.

(1 Peter 3:7-8 [New International Version])

WEEK 4:

We need patience to wait for that which is worth waiting for. God seldom does great things in a hurry. Continue to keep God first, stay prayed up, and have a blessed week.

²⁵But if we hope for what is still unseen by us, we wait for it with patience and composure.

(Romans 8:25 [Amplified Version])

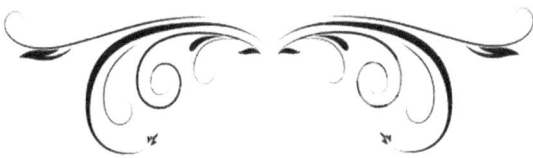

WEEK 5:

While we are nervously trying to figure things out, He (God), has already worked it out. Continue to keep God first, stay prayed up, and have a blessed week.

⁶So that we may boldly say, The LORD *is* my helper, and I will not fear what man shall do unto me.

(Hebrews 13:6 [King James Version])

WEEK 6:

It is so unfortunate when people use children to hurt one another because things do not go their way, or they cannot seem to get what they want. The LORD sees all and knows all. Stop being selfish and allow children to live their own lives. They are children. We as adults are supposed to nurture them and guide them. God is not pleased. Continue to keep God first, stay prayed up, and have a blessed week.

⁶Fathers do not irritate and provoke your children to anger, [do not exasperate them to resentment], but rear them [tenderly] in the training and discipline and the counsel and admonition of the LORD.

(Ephesians 6:4 [Amplified Version])

WEEK 7:

Anyone living without God in their lives is simply existing. Continue to keep God first, stay prayed up, and have a blessed week.

⁴Abide in me, and I in you. As the branch cannot bear fruit of itself, except it abide in the vine; no more can ye, except ye abide in me.

⁵ I am the vine, ye are the branches: He that abideth in me, and I in him, the same bringeth forth much fruit; for without me ye can do nothing.

(John 15:4-5 [King James Version])

WEEK 8:

It is unfortunate that some of us cannot see for looking and cannot hear for lack of listening. Check yourself first. Continue to keep God first, stay prayed up, and have a blessed week.

³Do nothing from selfishness or empty conceit, but with humility of mind regard one another as more important than yourselves. ⁴Do not merely look out for your own personal interests, but also for the interests of others.

(Philippians 2:3-4 [New American Standard Version])

WEEK 9:

When you are tempting to lose patience with someone, just remember how patient God has been with you. Continue to keep God first, stay prayed up, and have a blessed week.

⁸ The LORD is merciful and gracious, slow to anger, and plenteous in mercy.

(Psalms 103:8 [King James Version])

WEEK 10:

Do not pursue a heart that you are not ready to be loyal to. This includes loyalty to God. Continue to keep God first, stay prayed up, and have a blessed week.

²² Since by your obedience to the Truth *through the (Holy) Spirit* you have purified your hearts for the sincere affection of the brethren [see that you] love one another fervently from a pure heart.

(1 Peter 1:22 [Amplified Version])

WEEK 11:

Sometimes there are days when you just need a hug. Just because someone is smiling on the outside does not mean they are ok on the inside. Hug someone today just because. Continue to keep God first, stay prayed up, and have a blessed week.

¹⁸The Lord is near to the brokenhearted. And saves those who are crushed in spirit. ¹⁹Many are the afflictions of the righteous, but the LORD delivers him out of them all.

(Psalms 34:18-19 [New American Standard Version])

WEEK 12:

For those of us who do not think you have anything to be thankful for or did not give thanks today, if you are reading this message, you can see, you can read, and a whole lot of other things as well. Take life one day at a time, put *ALL* your burdens in God's hands, do not sweat the small stuff, and smile more. Continue to keep God first, stay prayed up, and have a blessed week.

¹⁵And let the peace of God rule in your hearts, to the which also ye are called in one body; and be ye thankful. ¹⁶Let the word of Christ dwell in you richly in all wisdom; teaching and admonishing one another in psalms and hymns and spiritual songs, singing with grace in your hearts to the Lord. ¹⁷And whatsoever ye do in word or deed, do all in the name of the Lord Jesus, giving thanks to God and the Father by him.

(Colossians 3:15-17 [King James Version])

WEEK 13:

It is easy to judge others. Sometimes we are so quick to put one another down rather than lift each other up. God puts us and others in one another's path for a reason and/or a season. Take time to just say hello, give a hug, pray with or for someone, make a phone call *(do not send a text),* or do something for someone without looking for anything in return. You never know, you could be someone's miracle. Continue to keep God first, stay prayed up, and have a blessed week.

¹¹Therefore encourage (admonish, exhort) one another and edify (strengthen and build up) one another, just as you are doing.

(1 Thessalonians 5:11 [Amplified Version])

WEEK 14:

Contrary to what we may have experienced in life, it is not hard to be happy. Take six months out of the year to take care of your own business and the other six months to leave other people's business along and that will keep you busy all year. In the meantime, love and spend time with family, do not let your job stress you out, and life can be good. More importantly, you must love that image that you see in the mirror. Continue to keep God first, stay prayed up, and have a blessed week.

¹**BLESSED** *is* the man that walketh not in the counsel of the ungodly, nor standeth in the way of sinners, nor sitteth in the seat of the scornful. ² But his delight is in the law of the LORD; and in his law doth he meditate day and night. ³ And he shall be like a tree planted by the rivers of water, that bringeth forth his fruit in his season; his leaf also shall not wither; and whatsoever he doeth shall prosper.

(Psalms 1:1-3 [King James Version])

WEEK 15:

There are some instances when we feel like someone is getting on our nerves, you do not want to be bothered with, or you just do not have time for. It is instances like this when your patience should kick in because that person could be you. Continue to keep God first, stay prayed up, and have a blessed week.

²⁹He that is slow to wrath is of great understanding; but he that is hasty of spirit exalteth folly.

(Proverbs 14:29 [King James Version])

WEEK 16:

Some of us do not realize that it is ok to say no and that some blessings that you receive from God is for you and you only. Continue to keep God first, stay prayed up, and have a blessed week.

³⁷Let your Yes be simply Yes, and your No be simply No; anything more than that comes from the evil one.

(Matthew 5:37 [Amplified Version])

WEEK 17:

Even when it is cloudy outside, it is still a beautiful day. You cannot have sunshine and not have rain. No matter what you are going through, tie a knot at the end of your rope and hang on for dear life because you only have one life to live. So, live it. Continue to keep God first, stay prayed up, and have a blessed week.

¹³I can do all things through Christ which strengtheneth me.

(Philippians 4:13 [King James Version])

WEEK 18:

Our words are powerful. We can use them to heal or harm, lift or lower, teach or taunt. Let us always be mindful of what we say and how we speak. Continue to keep God first, stay prayed up, and have a blessed week.

⁴A gentle tongue [with its healing power] is a tree of life, but willful contrariness in it breaks down the spirit.

(Proverbs 15:4 [Amplified Version])

WEEK 19:

Each day that we awaken is by the grace of God. It is an opportunity to start anew. God made life easy, we complicate our lives with the choices that we make. Continue to keep God first, stay prayed up, and have a blessed week.

⁸Do not let this Book of the Law depart from your mouth, meditate on it day and night, so that you may be careful to do everything written in it. Then you will be prosperous and successful.

(Joshua 1:8 [New International Version])

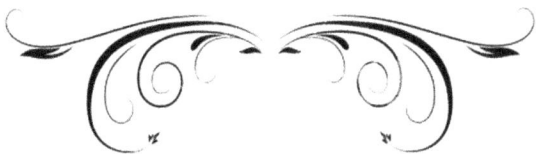

WEEK 20:

Focus on God's promises and not your problems. Continue to keep God first, stay prayed up, and have a blessed week.

¹⁰Fear thou not; for I *am* with thee: be not dismayed; for I *am* thy God: I will strengthen thee; yea, I will help thee; yea, I will uphold thee with the right hand of my righteousness.

(Isaiah 41:10 [King James Version])

WEEK 21:

Words have power that turns into actions that causes reactions. Depending on the words you speak, it will determine whether the outcome is positive or negative. Let us speak positive, encouraging words to one another. Continue to keep God first, stay prayed up, and have a blessed week.

⁴⁵ A good man out of the good treasure of his heart bringeth forth that which is good; and an evil man out of the evil treasure of his heart bringeth forth that which is evil: for abundance of the heart his mouth speaketh.

(Luke 6:45 [King James Version])

WEEK 22:

Are your mouth and mind saying and thinking two different things? Are you wondering why your prayers are not being answered? It is because the Lord knows our hearts. Let your mind, mouth, and heart be on one accord. Continue to keep God first, stay prayed up, and have a blessed week.

¹⁰I the LORD search the heart and examine the mind, to reward a man according to his conduct, according to what his deeds deserve.

(Jeremiah 17:10 [New International Version])

WEEK 23:

If you do not like what you see when you look in the mirror, then change it? Change it and make sure that the change is for you. It is you that must live with yourself each day. Continue to keep God first, stay prayed up, and have a blessed week.

¹⁷Therefore if any man be in Christ, he is a new creature; old things are passed away; behold, all things are become new.

(2 Corinthians 5:17 [King James Version])

WEEK 24:

Be the real you so that people will like you for real. Continue to keep God first, stay prayed up, and have a blessed week.

²⁵Therefore rejecting all falsity *and* being done now with it, let everyone express the truth with his neighbor, for we are all parts of one body *and* members one of another.

(Ephesians 4:25 [Amplified Version])

WEEK 25:

When you put God first, like who you see when you look in the mirror each morning and have a peace of mind when you lay down at night, everything else in between works out for the greater good. Continue to keep God first, stay prayed up, and have a blessed week.

³³But seek ye first the kingdom of God, and his righteousness; and all these things shall be added unto you.

(Matthew 6:33 [King James Version])

WEEK 26:

If you have tried everything and everyone, try God. You have nothing to lose and ***EVERYTHING*** to gain. He, (God), has an open-door policy but you must be the one to open the door and let Him in. Continue to keep God first, stay prayed up, and have a blessed week.

[19]Those whom I love I rebuke and discipline. So be earnest and repent. [20]Here I am! I stand at the door and knock. If anyone hears my voice and opens the door, I will come in and eat with him, and he with me.

(Revelation 3:19-20 [New International Version])

WEEK 27:

Need some help? Take it to the Lord in prayer and then stay out of the way and watch God work. He does not need any help. Continue to keep God first, stay prayed up, and have a blessed week.

²²Cast thy burden upon the LORD, and he shall sustain thee: he shall never suffer the righteous to be moved.

(Psalms 55:22 [King James Version])

WEEK 28:

There is nothing like family. Everyday should be like a family reunion. Let us love one another as God loves us. Continue to keep God first, stay prayed up, and have a blessed week.

⁷Beloved let us love one another, for love is from God; and everyone who loves is born of God and knows God. ⁸The one who does not love does not know God, for God is love. ⁹ By this the love of God was manifested in us, that God has sent His only begotten Son into the world so that we might live through Him.

(1 John 4:7-9 [New American Standard version])

WEEK 29:

Regardless of what you are going through, who you are going through it with, or how long, God is in control and things happen in God's timing and not ours. Continue to keep God first, stay prayed up, and have a blessed week.

¹¹For I know the plans I have for you, declares the LORD, plans to prosper you and not to harm you, plans to give you hope and a future.

(Jeremiah 29:11 [New International Version]

WEEK 30:

When you are going through hard times, dark times, and feel like you are going through the wilderness, just know that God knows what He is doing. Just be still. Continue to keep God first, stay prayed up, and have a blessed week.

¹⁴The LORD will fight for your, you need only to be still.

(Exodus 14:14 [New International Version])

WEEK 31:

If you are speaking out, reaching out, or trying to be understood but feel like it is falling on death ears, take ***EVERYTHING*** to the Lord in prayer. The best thing about it is, you can do it at ***ANY TIME*** and anywhere. God is always there… always. Continue to keep God first, stay prayed up, and have a blessed week.

¹²Then you will call upon me and come and pray to me, and I will listen to you. ¹³You will seek me and pray to me and find me when you seek me with all your heart.

(Jeremiah 29:12-13 [New International Version])

WEEK 32:

Prayer really works. Try it, go ahead. I dare you. I challenge you. Continue to keep God first, stay prayed up, and have a blessed week.

[24]Therefore I say unto you, What things soever ye desire, when ye pray, believe that ye receive *them*, and ye shall have *them*.

(Mark 11:24 [King James Version])

WEEK 33:

Imagine if everyone treated all others the way we wanted to be treated. How much better would the world be? Continue to keep God first, stay prayed up, and have a blessed week.

¹²So when, whatever you desire that others would do to *and* for you, even so do also to *and* for them, for this is (sums up) the Law and the Prophets.

(Matthew 7:12 [Amplified Version])

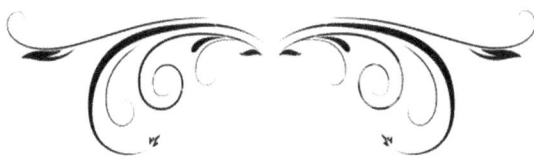

WEEK 34:

God is awesome, and He is a God of a second chance. If you have not tried Him, I dare you to do so. You have nothing to lose and everything to gain. Continue to keep God first, stay prayed up, and have a blessed week.

⁹ If we confess our sins, He is faithful and righteous to forgive us our sins and to cleanse us from all unrighteousness.

(1 John 1:9 [New American Standard Version])

WEEK 35:

Social media is a fast, easy way to communicate. Let us leave some things old school. Call your loved ones, visit, sit with the elderly, spend family time together with your children. One thing for sure that we can never get back is time and now-a-days, it is passing by so quickly. Continue to keep God first, stay prayed up, and have a blessed week.

²⁴And let us consider *and* give attentive, continuous care to watching over one another, studying how we may stir up to love *and* helpful deeds *and* noble activities. ²⁵Not forsaking or neglecting to assemble together as in the habit of some people, but admonishing on another, and all the more faithfully as ye se the day approaching.

(Hebrews 10: 24-25 [Amplified Version])

WEEK 36:

Do not compare your life to anyone else. God has a purpose for us all. Find your purpose and live it. If you do not know what your purpose is, seek God for the answer. Continue to keep God first, stay prayed up, and have a blessed week.

²¹Many are the plans in a man's heart, but it is the LORD's purpose that prevails.

(Proverbs 19:21 [New International Version])

WEEK 37:

God is in the blessing business so get you some business with God. Continue to keep God first, stay prayed up, and have a blessed week.

⁸But you shall remember the LORD your God, for it is He who gives you the ability to produce wealth, and so confirms His covenant, which He swore to your ancestors, as it is today.

(Deuteronomy 8:18 [Amplified Version])

WEEK 38:

We as human beings are leaving this world in alarming rates. Take the time to say hello, thank you, please, I am sorry, and I love you on a daily basis because we know not what tomorrow may bring. And if you are holding a grudge, let it go. Start today. Continue to keep God first, stay prayed up, and have a blessed week.

⁴Be kind to one another, tender-hearted, forgiving each other, just as God in Christ also has forgiven you.

(Ephesians 4:32 [New American Standard Version]

WEEK 39:

You have not because you ask not. Ask boldly for what you will of God. Ask, believe, and expect with humility and watch God show up and show out. Continue to keep God first, stay prayed up, and have a blessed week.

⁷Ask, and it shall be given you; seek, and ye shall find; knock, and it shall be opened unto you: ⁸For everyone that asketh receiveth; and he that seeketh findeth; and to him that knocketh it shall be opened.

(Matthew 7:7-8 [King James Version])

WEEK 40:

Do you love yourself? When you do, it allows you to love others without being selfish, without doubt, without jealousy, and even unconditionally just to name a few. Look in the mirror and do a self-evaluation. Continue to keep God first, stay prayed up, and have a blessed week.

¹⁴Let everything be done in love (true love to God and man as inspired by God's love to us.

(1 Corinthians 16:14 [Amplified Version])

WEEK 41:

How can you expect others to like you for who you are when you are pretending to be something or someone that you are not? Just be yourself so you can be liked and loved for the "real" you. Continue to keep God first, stay prayed up, and have a blessed week.

⁴For there is not man that doeth anything in secret, and he himself seeketh to be known openly. If thou do these things, show thyself to the world.

(John 7:4 [King James Version])

WEEK 42:

Beauty is in the eye of the beholder. Make sure your beauty comes from the inside and you will not have to worry about the outside. Continue to keep God first, stay prayed up, and have a blessed week.

³Your beauty should not come from outward adornment, such as braided hair and the wearing of gold jewelry and fine clothes.

⁴Instead, it should be that of inner self, the unfading beauty of a gentle and quiet spirit which is of great worth in God's sight.

(1 Peter 3:3-4 [New International Version])

WEEK 43:

There is nothing worse than not having a peace of mind in your own home. If there is something that is not right, allow God to be in the midst and watch Him fix it. Continue to keep God first, stay prayed up, and have a blessed week.

⁴And the peace of God, which surpasses all comprehension, will guard your hearts and your minds in Christ Jesus.

(Philippians 4:7 [New American Standard Version])

WEEK 44:

If you do not like what you see in the mirror, change it even if others will not like it. *"You"* are the one that has to live with *"yourself"* daily. If you need help making that change, take it to the Lord in prayer. Continue to keep God first, stay prayed up, and have a blessed week.

¹³I can do all things through Christ who strengthens me.

(Philippians 4:13 [King James Version])

WEEK 45:

You can only live for today because yesterday is gone, and tomorrow will have issues of its own. So, live for today, love today, and be happy today and let God take care of the rest. Continue to keep God first, stay prayed up, and have a blessed week.

³⁴So do not worry *or* be anxious about tomorrow, for tomorrow will have worries *and* anxieties of its own. Sufficient for each day is its own trouble.

(Matthew 6:34 [Amplified Version])

WEEK 46:

Be true to yourself so you can be true to others. Continue to keep God first, stay prayed up, and have a blessed week.

⁸I am not speaking this as a command, but as providing through the earnestness of others the sincerity of your love also.

(2 Corinthians 8:8 [New American Standard Version])

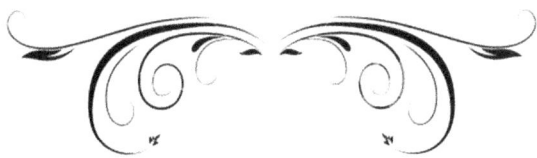

WEEK 47:

Sometimes when we intend to help, we become part of the problem by hindering the person or persons that need help. Sometimes we must step back and just pray about the situation which only God can fix anyway. It is ok. Unfortunately, we cannot help everyone that needs help, but God can. So, step back and let God do what He does best. After all, He is God, and He does not need any help. Continue to keep God first, stay prayed up, and have a blessed week.

¹²For the word of God is living and active. Sharper than any double-edged sword, it penetrates even to dividing soul and spirit, joints and marrow; it judges the thoughts and attitudes of the heart.

(Hebrews 4:12 [New International Version])

WEEK 48:

Everyday should be considered Mother's Day. Let us not take just one day out of the year to celebrate our mothers. Spend time with her, hug her, and tell her you love her as often as possible. Continue to keep God first, stay prayed up, and have a blessed week.

⁸My son, listen to the instructions of thy father, and forsake not the law of thy mother. ⁹For they shall be an ornament of grace unto thy head, and chains about thy neck.

(Proverbs 1:8-9 [King James Version])

²⁰Children obey your parents in all things: for this is wellpleasing unto the Lord.

(Colossians 3:20 [King James Version])

WEEK 49:

Even when it is cloudy outside, it is still a beautiful day. We cannot have sunshine and not have rain. No matter what you are going through, tie a knot at the end of your rope and hang on for dear life because you only have one life to live. So, live it. Continue to keep God first, stay prayed up, and have a blessed week.

24 This *is* the day *which* the LORD hath made; we will rejoice and be glad in it.

(Psalms 118:24 [King James Version])

WEEK 50:

Whatever the season, God gets the glory for it all. Be thankful and grateful for all things. Continue to keep God first, stay prayed up, and have a blessed week.

[20]Now to him who is able to do immeasurably more than all we ask or imagine, according to his power that is at work within us. [21]to him be glory in the church and in Christ Jesus throughout all generations. For ever and ever! Amen

(Ephesians 3:20-21 [New International Version])

WEEK 51:

Want a legitimate, spirit filled hook-up? Talk to God. He has something for EVERYONE! Continue to keep God first, stay prayed up, and have a blessed week.

³Commit thy works unto the LORD, and thy thoughts shall be established.

(Proverbs 16:3 [King James Version])

WEEK 52:

Being honest is not difficult at all. Integrity is doing the right thing for the right reasons. It is part of free will that God gave us. Continue to keep God first, stay prayed up, and have a blessed week.

"A Thought for the Week"

⁹The man of integrity walks securely, but he who takes crooked paths will be found out.

(Proverbs 10:9 [New International Version])

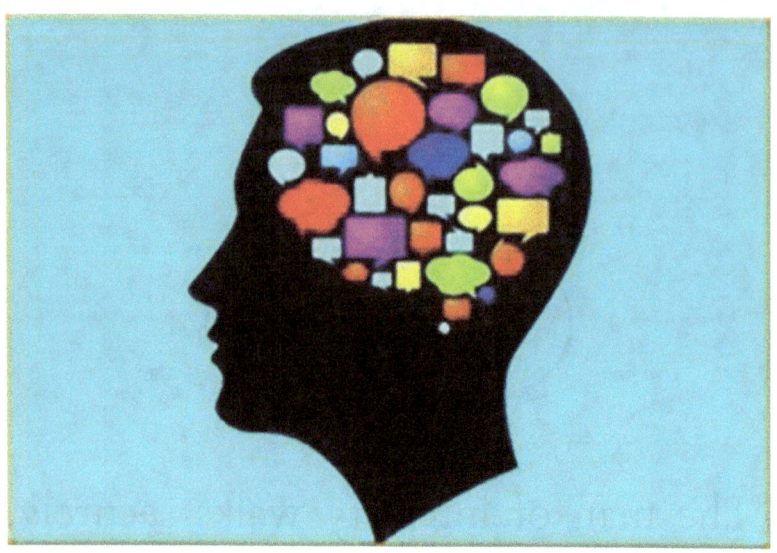

Life for most have become more hectic with all the changes and adjustments that we had to make with work, school, raising our families and life in general due to COVID-19. It became difficult to maintain positive thoughts with the loss of so many lives worldwide. Trying to maintain a positive attitude, support from others, and a lot of prayers is what got us through the tough times.

We all are still working to make it better and get back to some type of normalcy. In this book, I am sharing some positive thoughts along with scripture to support those thoughts. These thoughts can be utilized to get your week started on a positive note.

There are 52 weeks in a year. And I am excited that you do not have to start the book at the beginning. You can start on whatever the week it is during the year that you receive the book and enjoy it throughout the year.

It is my hope that this *Collection of 52 Inspirational Thoughts for the Week* is a true blessing to you in thought and in spirit. So, I challenge you to *stay prayed up, continue to keep God first, and have a blessed week* each week throughout the year.